I Feel Sad

By Connor Stratton

level 2

little blue readers

www.littlebluehousebooks.com

Little Blue House is distributed by North Star Editions:
sales@northstareditions.com | 888-417-0195

Produced for Little Blue House by Red Line Editorial.

Photographs ©: Shutterstock Images, cover, 10–11, 12, 15, 16–17, 18, 21; iStockphoto, 4, 6–7, 9, 22–23, 24 (top left), 24 (top right), 24 (bottom left), 24 (bottom right)

Library of Congress Control Number: 2020913845

ISBN
978-1-64619-299-1 (hardcover)
978-1-64619-317-2 (paperback)
978-1-64619-353-0 (ebook pdf)
978-1-64619-335-6 (hosted ebook)

Printed in the United States of America
Mankato, MN
012021

About the Author

Connor Stratton enjoys writing books for children and watching movies, such as *Inside Out*. He's always trying to understand his feelings better. He lives in Minnesota.

Table of Contents

Why I'm Sad

Sometimes I feel sad.

I miss my family, and

that's why I'm sad.

I hurt my knee, and that's why I'm sad.

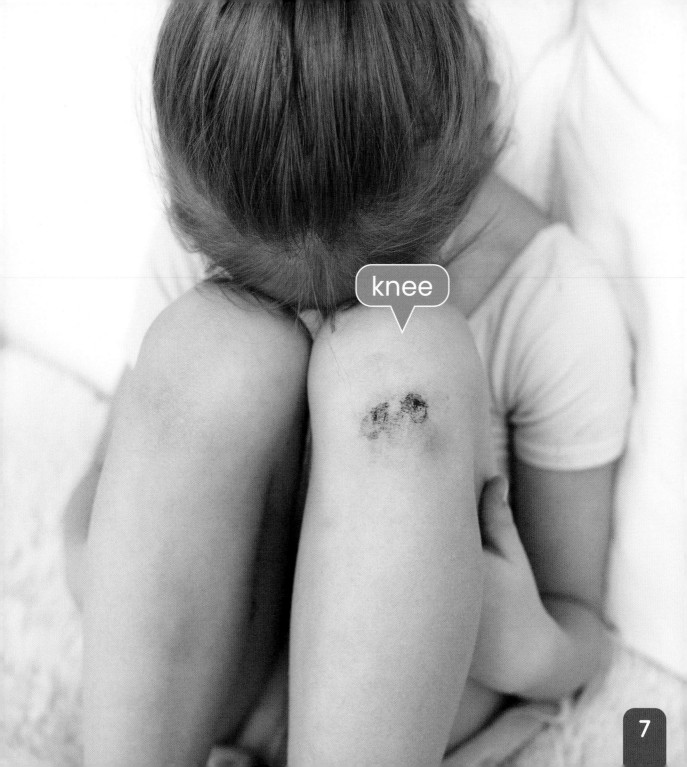

My toy broke, and that's why I'm sad.

toy

My friends were mean,
and that's why I'm sad.
It's not fun to feel sad.

friends

What I Do

I do different things
when I'm sad.
I feel sad, so I sit
on my own.

I feel sad, so I put my head in my hands.

I feel sad, so I cry.

It's okay to feel sad.

Feeling Better

I tell my mom and dad.

I tell them I am sad.

My dad hugs me.

He holds me tight.

I take deep breaths, and
I feel better.